The Woman's Field Guide
to Exceptional Living

"I have come to believe that the main task of each of us perfectly imperfect humans is to remember: there are always fresh possibilities to be discovered, we are always loved, we are part of the Whole. Corrie offers exactly the kind of splendid playful reminders I need."

>Jennifer Louden,
>author of *The Woman's Comfort Book*
>and *The Life Organizer*
>www.jenniferlouden.com

"Corrie provides a powerful call to action and simple solutions to begin today. Pick up the book and prepare to be inspired."

>Wanda Urbanska, President/Host of
>"Simple Living with Wanda Urbanska"
>television series
>www.simplelivingtv.net

"This field guide to being a woman is inspired. It is a powerful resource for making a good life great. Don't leave home without it!"

Helene Van Manen,
MCC Master Certified Coach
www.coachhelene.com

"A fun, thought-provoking little book you'll want to revisit often! Written with a light hearted, yet soulful style, it's thoroughly engaging, inspiring, and uplifting."

Carol McClelland, Ph.D.,
author of *The Seasons of Change*
www.transitiondynamics.com

"Corrie Woods offers an irresistible invitation and resourceful guide to living a life boldly, creatively, and happily. She provides a wealth of ideas, practices, and tools that are inspirational, practical, and motivational. This book makes a life-affirming and positive contribution to any reader!"

Angeles Arrien, Ph.D.
Cultural Anthropologist
author of *The Four-Fold Way*
and *Signs of Life*
www.angelesarrien.com

the
Woman's
Field Guide™

to

Exceptional
Living

Practical Steps for
Living a Big, Bold, Beautiful Life!

the
Woman's
Field Guide™

to

Exceptional Living

Practical Steps for
Living a Big, Bold, Beautiful Life!

Corrie Woods

New York

The Woman's Field Guide™ to Exceptional Living
©2008 by Corrie Woods

Editorial: Maureen Smith
Interior Design: Liz Tufte, Folio Bookworks www.folio-bookworks.com
Illustration: Caren Frost Olmsted, CFO Design www.cfodesign.com
Cover Design: Kathi Dunn, Dunn+Associates www.dunn-design.com
Author Photo: Lynne Siler

Publisher's Cataloging-in-Publication Data
Woods, Corrie, 1959–
   The woman's field guide™ to exceptional living: practical steps for
   living a big, bold, beautiful life / Corrie Woods. – Tryon, NC:
   Barefoot Wisdom Press, ©2007.

      p. : ill. ; cm.
      ISBN: 978-1-60037-395-4

   1. Women–Conduct of life. 2. Women–Life skills guides.
   3. Self-realization in women. 4. Quality of life. I. Title.

HQ2037.W66 2007
646.70082–dc22

                                                            0709

Published by:

MORGAN · JAMES
THE ENTREPRENEURIAL PUBLISHER™
www.morganjamespublishing.com

Part of the MegaBook Series

Morgan James Publishing, LLC
1225 Franklin Ave. Ste 325
Garden City, NY 11530-1693
Toll Free 800-485-4943
www.MorganJamesPublishing.com

Habitat
for Humanity®
Peninsula
Building Partner

To my father, John Woods, who was the ultimate life coach for his friends, colleagues, and his family.

To my mother, Loti Woods, whose strength, wisdom, and enduring love inspire her three daughters each and every day.

To my two cherished children: Kipling and Chelsea — a son and a daughter who have taught me far more than I have ever hoped to teach them. What a blessed parent am I.

And to Jay, an amazing man who has taught me the joys of living life with a wide-open heart. His steadfast support and encouragement helped me to bring this book to life.

Acknowledgements

The writing of this book has been a joyful, creative adventure every step of the way. A huge part of that joy has come from collaborations with others. Some thank you's go far beyond words. For each person I shall mention, this is the case. I like to think the biggest thank you will come down the road, as we join up to play with future projects.

I approached Caren Frost Olmsted about illustrating this book when it was a tiny seed of an idea ready to sprout. With all her creative genius in motion, she brought to life the energy, heart, and playfulness I felt in the writing of the words. Co-creating with Caren is the best!

To my generous *word stewards* who helped in a variety of ways to craft and polish a finished work: Maureen Smith, editor, friend, advisor, caring shoulder; Bobbi Sommers, providing fresh eyes at just the right time; Betsy Gory, whose insights have helped me to become a better writer; Cynthia Williams and Miranda Miller for critical final touches.

To my *technical book stewards*: Kathi and Hobie with Dunn & Associates; Liz at Folio Bookworks; Graham and Susan at Write to Your Market; to Mission Publishing; to Dan Poynter.

To my mentors, coaches, and dear friends: you each inspire me in the way you show up in the world. There are not enough words! Helene Van Manen, Doug Silsbee, Denise Hedges.

To those who, through their own works and contributions, have unwittingly contributed to who I am and to the writing of this book: Jennifer Louden, Susan Jeffers, Wanda Urbanksa, Carol McClelland, Joan Borysenko, Angeles Arriens, Cheri Britton, Elizabeth Barbour, Sarah Benoit, Maggie Butler, Claire Mandeville.

To two women whose gifts came to me in very special packages: Peggy Tabor Millin who helped me put pen to paper after a very long dry spell; Marilyn McGuire who helped me transform a collection of loose words into a book by saying just the right thing at just the right time.

And finally, a special thank you to the women of the *Savvy Savory Self-Care Retreat* and to my clients, current and past. What a joy to share in the discoveries of living exceptional lives together!

Contents

Introduction

The seed of this book was planted a few years back by a man I adored. My grandfather held a special place in my heart. I am not sure if it was the stories he wove of days gone by, the North Carolina patch of heaven that he and my grandmother tended and I loved to visit, or the captivating sparkle in his eyes.

On one remarkable day, a few precious words he shared changed my life. As he held my hand, he smiled and said, "Corrie, I have lived a great life. If I had it to do over again, I wouldn't change a thing." Those were the last words he would share with me.

In that moment I felt like I was being handed a torch to carry forward – a torch that blazed with the words: Wake up! Don't miss another minute of your life! Live it! Love it! And when your days are ended you will be able to smile and say, "If I had my life to live over again I wouldn't change a thing. No regrets!" This was the proverbial wake-up call of my life. It rang out loud and clear. The path I have followed, from that day to this, led to the writing of this guidebook. It is my heart's way of continuing to pass the torch along.

It is in that spirit that I share this book. As you read through the pages, cover-to-cover, or pick and choose pertinent sections, notice what resonates with you, what calls you out to play, what invites deeper inquiry. There may be rich memories that rise up and beckon you to dust them off, brand new insights that stir your excitement, or even a few sticky spots that grab your attention. Along the way, you will find invitations to move beyond reading the pages by engaging in the experience at hand. The Field Notes pages invite you to pause with the chapter, to take out a pen and journal to the prompts provided, or to whatever has bubbled up for you. With the turn of each page, the opportunities are ripe for you to identify and embrace the many facets of a well-lived and well-loved life.

It is my intention for you to play and allow the following pages to guide you onto a path of more vibrant living.

Setting Your Inner Compass To Yes!

A BOLD Woman –

A Brilliant, Outrageous, Luminary Diva

We've been playing small for far too long.
We've been "toning it down" and shrinking
so that others won't feel uncomfortable around us.
Debrena Jackson Gandy

As I look back on my life, my juiciest memories come in waves when I revisit moments that I stretched myself, showed up with a burst of courage, tried on a new hat, stepped off the well-worn path, or set out in a new direction. Think about your most vivid memories. Wouldn't you agree?

When was the last time a stretch took you into new territory? It is ever so easy to find yourself in early retirement from your life. Your days become routine, the same thoughts recycle over and over, and your actions are executed within the narrow groove of what's familiar. Those peak moments become few and far between and you wonder why life starts feeling flat. When you find yourself facing such a quandary, it is time to take action, pump some new blood into your veins, and seek out new vistas.

Perhaps you are shaking in your boots when you hear the word "bold." It may conjure up thoughts like daredevil, risk, uncertainty. Rest easy. If you are intrepid when you think about stretching, know that you get to define what a great stretch is *for you*. Start by thinking about what your routine looks like and do something different. Drive a new route to work, try eating something you have never tasted before, or wear a flashy new color. Start with small steps.

Fan the flames and build momentum for taking bold action

One facet of living an exceptional life is feeling the energy, thrill, and inspiration that are ushered in with your bold, stretch experiences. Reminding yourself of that energy may coax you, or even propel you, to invite more juicy, bold moments into your day, into your life.

From your memory bank, pull up those moments in your life when you stretched, took a bold leap, or dipped an excited toe into the edge of a new pond. Stay with those memories for a spell and allow them to ripple through you. Next, move into the feelings that accompany the memories.

A few things to keep in mind

- You cannot think your way to bold living. It comes with actions, large or small, so get out of your head.

- Be willing to act as intuition pops up, as you feel the nudge. Be willing to be playfully spontaneous!

- Be willing to be surprised, and further, be willing to feel a bit (or a lot) foolish.

- When you step outside your comfort zone, it can feel edgy. Know with that edge comes personal growth.

- Hand-in-hand with bold living comes living a life of no regrets. How cool is that?

Powerful questions can stir the pot and break down barriers that hold you back.

Here are a few you might explore:

Have you taken early retirement in your life?

What assumptions or fears may get in the way of your being a bit more adventurous as you move through each day?

What are the benefits for you in stretching more often in your life?

From whom do you need to get permission to begin the shift?

A call to action

And now for the fun part! What bold action would you love to take? Make your list.

Skinny dip! Try a new sport. Take a friend on an extraordinary picnic. Sign up for a class, workshop, or retreat that provides a great stretch. Play with a flashy new look. Try something (anything) you have always wanted to do but were afraid to try. Go for a drive in the countryside and follow the road wherever it leads. Climb a mountain. Travel to a foreign country. Travel with the spirit of adventure to an unexplored place just down the road.

Begin today. Step outside your comfortable groove, explore, invite surprises, and you will quickly become a more energized you!

Get fired up to play, and play big, and the lights sparkling around you will say: Here is a BOLD Woman – a Brilliant, Outrageous, Luminary Diva!

Field Notes

When I think back to times I have been BOLD in
my life, this is what comes to mind:

Field Notes

Get out some colored pencils or crayons and list, in big, bright colors, things you will be doing to step up the BOLD in your life.

Make Your Life a Celebration

Everything is created from
moment to moment, always new.
Like fireworks, this universe is a celebration and
you are the spectator contemplating the eternal
Fourth of July of your absolute splendor.
— Francis Lucille

When you think of celebrations and rituals, what comes to mind? Religious services, birthdays, anniversaries? We celebrate and have rituals around the obvious, yet there are so many events, passages, and experiences that stand out as significant in our lives. Recognize significant moments by taking time, through ritual or celebration, and you will deepen your experience, create powerful memories, and reap profound rewards. You will transform moments and experiences that might have been missed, in the quick passage of time, into sacred milestones.

Some ordinary and extraordinary opportunities for celebration

A move to a new city or new land, the birth of a baby, saying goodbye to a loved one, a winter solstice, the first bloom of spring, a *great* new success in your professional life, an interesting new friend arriving at your door, the words *I forgive you*, the words *I forgive me*, a girls' night out, a fabulous blunder that leads to a fabulous insight, completing a big project, running your first mile, or running your first marathon.

Though I am not a person who gets into an "another day older" kind of panic when my birthday rolls around, the year my fortieth approached I felt it was time to shake things up a bit. I booked a flight to Riverton, Wyoming, and headed off with a new backpack and a bold heart on a solo adventure into the Wind River Range. I was following a call to celebrate a passage in my life in a way that set the stage and extended an invitation for what was to come.

In another vein, my friend Helen came up with a creative way of celebrating a personal victory. One day she noticed that she had begun saying YES, when her old way may have been to let fear lead with the words NO. Conversely, she had begun saying NO when her former accommodating self would have pushed past her boundaries and said YES. Wow! She noticed she was showing up for herself in a gutsy new ways. She didn't just stop with the noticing, though. Helen wanted to share her success and her news. How might she celebrate? Gathering together a few dear friends, she threw a YES/NO party. With her creative spirit charged up, she set the stage for play by crafting a simple game that led to lots of laughter and rich conversation. The game included a handful of cards with thought-provoking questions, a tasty treat for each answer given, and a prize for everyone as the party wrapped up. Her friends had a blast. They could relate to the theme, and were inspired by her enthusiastic celebration to look at how YES/NO show up in their own lives. For Helen, this playful celebration reinforced an exciting moment of growth in her life and gave her a powerful touchstone to refer back to.

Look around you. Look at your life. How much time do you spend focused on the next challenge or problem? When you fail to take time for reflection and celebration, you end up with a "what's next mentality" and the real gems slip past unnoticed. Ah, that is the real value of ritual and celebration. You intentionally take time to savor, to make sacred, and to relish. It can support closure or pop the lid on something new. Further, it can create a rich, powerful memory to cherish for a lifetime.

Translate celebration into valuable new life skills that might include:

- A greater ability to savor special moments in your life.

- Experiencing times of change and passages in a more thoughtful way.

- Becoming more resourceful in releasing and moving on.

- Maintaining an intentional focus on causes for celebration rather than on moments of defeat or struggle.

- Embodying a deeper sense of celebration throughout your life.

Let me repeat that last one:
*Embodying a deeper sense of celebration
throughout your life!*

Wow! How great would that feel, and more importantly, how do you get there? Simple – it begins one celebration at a time!

Field Notes

Pick one cause for celebration and Celebrate!

Field Notes

How might I begin living a
life of celebration today?

The Gifts of Gratitude

Feeling gratitude and not expressing it is like
wrapping a present and not giving it.
—*William Arthur Ward*

What if you began and ended each day with an expression of gratitude for the blessings in your life? Through prayer, journaling, or a phone call, how might that intentional ritual affect the quality of each day? What if each experience of gratitude was like a drop into the pool of your life, sending ripples in all directions? How far might those ripples spread? In contrast, what if gratitude was an infrequent blip on the radar or it was expressed only in times traditionally recognized as occasions to "give thanks"? How would that lack of gratitude impact your life? If I were to name one thing that has transformed my life, hands down it would be a deep experience of gratitude.

In one of the darkest moments in my life, I began a practice of gratitude. It served as a lifeline, pulling me toward the light. At that particular time, I could have endlessly thought about what was not working in my life. I could have moaned and declared to the Universe that I was justified to complain. But it occurred to me when I did, that I only felt worse, and I seemed to perpetuate the hardship and pain.

stop complaining

The shift into grateful living began simply, one intentional word, one feeling at a time. It was as if I planted seeds, and each day I watered the seeds with my words, intentions, and feelings. Now my life has grown into a bountiful garden, filled with color and amazing possibilities.

one seed at a time...

So, what is Gratitude? A response of your heart. A feeling of thankfulness and appreciation. Think about your life in this moment. Perhaps you could fill endless pages with glowing words of appreciation; perhaps it is difficult to get past a blank page. Whether you are experiencing one of life's brilliant pinnacles or slowly traversing a dark void, *you* get to choose. You may choose a feeling of lack or a feeling of abundance, choose a state of complaint or a state of gratitude.

Here is the edge that comes when you complain: no matter how much you complain, you never feel satisfied. As each word flows out of your mouth, it is as if you are greasing a slide that takes you farther down into discontent. I love the words of Wayne Dyer when he writes about being a love-finder rather than a fault-finder. Are you focusing on what is not working in your life or are you focusing on what is? The reality is that we all have some of both. What sets some folks apart, with a sparkle in their eye and a generous heart, is that they live their life as a love-finder. The ripples from their grateful heart can be felt by everyone around them.

focus?

The rewards of feeling a deep sense of gratitude are extraordinary. You will feel more joyful, more attractive, more vibrant, more satisfied, and more present to giving and receiving love.

Now take a deep breath, settle yourself for a moment and then complete the following sentence, which will help you begin, right this moment, your shift into more grateful living.

I feel so very grateful for . . .

It is that easy. Now let's really dive in to play.

- Brainstorm ten outside-the-box ideas of ways you can express your gratitude to others. Watch the people in your life unfold into big smiles when you express just how very grateful you are. Be creative in that expression.

- Write a gratitude letter to yourself or to someone you know.

- Make a list of fifty things you are grateful for and keep it handy to look at when you find yourself sliding into a complaining mode.

- Create a Gratitude Journal. Set aside time everyday to think about, to feel, and to write down what you are grateful for.

- Be open to listening to the language of your heart.

What a gift to feel a big open heart, to bask in your blessings, to choose consciously, intentionally to live a life of gratitude. Let gratitude ripple within you and joyfully out into your world.

Field Notes

I am so very grateful for . . .

Field Notes

A new daily gratitude practice for me is . . .

Stand in the Spotlight

"If what others thought of you wasn't important – if the only thing that mattered was how your heart felt about your life – what would you be doing differently?"
– Melody Beattie

Just imagine, the stage curtains are drawn and you are standing backstage, alone in the darkness. The house is full. Anticipation is building. You feel butterflies in your stomach. You know when the curtains open, a magnificent woman will be revealed standing center stage, in the spotlight, fully expressed. And, frankly, the thought terrifies you.

What does fully expressed really mean? A word that comes to mind is authentic. According to The *Merriam-Webster Dictionary,* authentic means: *true to one's own personality, spirit, or character.*

To live authentically means that you truly hold nothing back. You believe in who you are and the gifts you have to share. Yet, as simple as this might sound, there are countless reasons people have difficulty living authentically, difficulty showing up in full color, difficulty being fully expressed.

My awareness of my tendency to show up as "less than" grew out of a handful of words shared by an insightful support person in my life. For all the fabulous things that I had going on in my life, for all that I was being and becoming that I was proud of, his questions went something like this: *Corrie, in what ways are you holding back from really showing up? How and where do you reduce your presence in the world?*

I realized in an instant, given how deeply those words resonated, that he was onto something.

My line of exploration and inquiry evolved over time and began with:

In what ways am I holding back?

And on to:

What am I afraid of?

And finally:

What steps can I take to jump onto center stage in my life and stand in the spotlight beaming, as a fully expressed woman?

What an evolution this began and what a change this brought to my life and to who I am becoming!

There are barriers many women face that stand in the way of courageously, joyfully showing up. The four most common blocks – The Four Big Bullies – are:

the should
the have to
the yeah but
the I'll get around to it when.

The ability to knock these obstacles down, one by one, comes first with noticing *how* they present themselves in your life. By noticing and naming these culprits, you build your awareness. That is step one to effective change.

The Should: I should be more like so and so. I should look different. I should consider other people's needs before my own.

The Have To: I have to work in this job I hate. I have to avoid touchy subjects with so and so. I have to do countless things I really do not enjoy and that's life.

The Yeah-but: Yeah-but, I am too out of shape to get into shape. Yeah-but, I am too old to get hired for a great job.

The I'll get around to it when: I'll get around to eating a better diet when the holidays have passed. I'll get around to managing my finances when I get caught up. I'll get around to writing that important letter when I finish up the things on my To Do List.

The roles you perform in response to these nasty bullies, the masks you wear when interacting with the outside world, and the time you spend putting off real joy gets in the way of living a fully expressed life on your own terms. Over time, you may find the person you have crafted is a far cry from who you really are.

In time you *can* return home. In time you *can* set masks aside. In time you can celebrate landing the role of a lifetime – that of being your glorious, authentic self. How to prepare for this staring role in your life?

- Remove the masks. Notice in what ways you may be showing up as someone else or for someone else in your life. Take off those masks that get in the way of your authentic expression and put them on the shelf.

- Practice extraordinary self-care. Be number one on your own priority list and commit to taking great care of yourself so that when the curtains open, you will be beaming with pride and confidence.

- Get clear about your gifts. We all have unique and stunning gifts to give. Perhaps you can teach, offer a helping hand, share a warm and caring heart, or present a fresh perspective that leads to new solutions. Step far away from what you should do and identify what makes your heart sing. Acknowledge and embrace your gifts and then share them with the world.

- Choose your support circle wisely. Be prepared to put some distance between yourself and those who do not support you showing up in all your glory.

It takes guts to stand in the spotlight, but the rewards are rich: greater joy, no regrets, expressing your passions rather than holding them at bay, the flood of incredible people who show up to play with you because your light is shining far and wide. Take center stage, completely expressed in your life, and you will find that the rewards last a lifetime.

Begin crafting a new script today with yourself in the starring role. When you commit to live authentically, the curtains will open wide for you. There will be no more hiding backstage in the shadows. As you proudly take your place on center stage in the spotlight, your gifts to the world will be revealed, the audience will cheer, and you will have the time of your life!

Some of my favorite fully expressed women

Helene Van Manen
http://www.coachhelene.com

Jennifer Louden
http://www.jenniferlouden.com

Sandra Magsamen
http://www.sandramagsamen.com/

Jean Shinoda Bolen, M.D.
http://www.jeanbolen.com/

Cheri Britton
http://www.boomthinking.com/

Susan Jeffers, Ph.D.
http://www.susanjeffers.com

I invite you to learn more about them!

Field Notes

A post-it kind of day:

In what ways are you showing up as less than your glorious self? Carry with you a pad of post-its and jot down any time you notice yourself holding back, not fully expressing yourself. Stick them all right here and in a couple of days come back to look at what you have written. Interesting?

Field Notes

Banish the Bullies:

Each time you notice one pop up,

transform your language in that moment.

Self-Courtship –
Love Thy Self

*"Love is what you naturally express when you are
comfortable and confident in your own skin.
You don't have to earn or deserve love."*
— Rhonda Britten

My earliest memories of flowers are woven out of the sweet scent of spring, a cool Sunday morning, and a batch of lily-of-the-valleys blooming just outside the kitchen door. I loved those flowers. They seemed the most beautiful, delicate, inviting pieces of nature I had ever experienced.

Today, highest on my list of self-care gestures is the simple act of filling my home with flowers. It feels a bit like courting, romancing myself.

Though a vase of fresh flowers may not be significant to one person, to another it may be nurturing and beautiful and put a smile on their face. A cornerstone of living an exceptional life is feeling and expressing self-love. Let self-courtship become an intentional act you perform each and every day. It may be as simple as a bouquet of wild-flowers or a hot bath or an intentional deep breath in the midst of a whirlwind.

Why is this practice so very important? You can get to the answer in a roundabout way. Are you familiar with the experience of trying to get clear about something, struggling with a big decision, or feeling the frustration of living life as a juggling act? These and similar experiences lead to a sense of disconnection from yourself and those you love. When you are faced with difficult challenges and difficult feelings, often the response is to work harder to overcome them. It's the direct-attack kind of approach.

A more indirect approach might look like this: step away from the issue at hand. Place it tempo-rarily on hold and focus on one thing only – filling your self-care cup to overflowing. It seems coun-terintuitive, but think about it. If you nurture yourself, give yourself lots of breathing room, take time to play and to smile a bit, you become more resourceful. Once-elusive solutions appear and you find yourself with the energy and skill to handle most everything. Couple this with feeling nurtured, rested, connected, and pampered and you will find that the benefits of self-love are boundless.

Prime your self-love pump
What things can you do for yourself to say, "I love you?"

- Write yourself a love letter. Sound silly? That's OK. Put pen to paper to honor yourself and celebrate the gift of who you are.

- Smile at yourself each time you catch your reflection in the mirror.

- Buy yourself flowers.

- Take that nice hot bubble bath.

- Say "yes" when your heart says "yes" and "no" when it says "no."

Pamper yourself!
Nurture yourself!
Be creative!

Surprise yourself!

Living life without self-courtship has a high cost.
We risk losing our sensuality, our senses, precious
moments with those we love, our smile, and our joy.
When we romance ourselves, it prepares a fertile
garden for a profusion of love to bloom in all areas
of our lives. We regain passion and *now* becomes a
moment not to be missed!

Dear Beloved,

It seems silly and a bit awkward to be writing to you. I know so well how to thank and praise and adore my family and friends. Giving thanks and expressing love to you, well, honestly it will take a bit of getting used to.

Perhaps I can start here . . . what if I expressed the love to you that I express to others? How might that look? How might that feel?

I might buy myself some flowers . . .

Yes, I'll go to the florist and pick bud for bud the ones that delight my eye. Then I will fill up a vase and sit beside this flower canvas and breathe and smile and doze and do whatever my heart guides me to do.

Ah, that is indeed a starting place.

I do love and honor you so.

Your beloved,
Me

Field Notes

What is the price I, and those I love,
pay when I am not loving myself?

Field Notes

Create a Self-Courtship coin jar.
When it is full, do something special just for you!

Trailblazing the Experience of Your Life

Crafting a Personal Retreat

"A woman's retreat springs from and is guided by a woman's inner knowing. A woman's retreat is about stepping out of your ordinary existence to listen and attune to your truest, most authentic self. It is about being self-referenced to become self-restored."
— Jennifer Louden

Retreat: a place and time for you to get reacquainted with you; the ebb in *ebb and flow;* a solitary sanctuary for renewal; a safe haven; a snug den, a refuge.

Retreat is both an experience and a state of mind. It can be a time of journaling and deep contemplation, of simply being and seeing what comes up, or of a deep connective experience in nature. Is a personal retreat a weekend away from the family and friends or thirty minutes created with care in the middle of a busy day? It can be both. A personal retreat is crafted and defined by you. Do you long for mini-retreats sprinkled throughout your week? Does a day or weekend away from the familiar call to you? What about an evening retreat under star-light or in the glow of candlelight? Or perhaps you are scratching your head and thinking, *I have never even considered taking this kind of time just for me.*

Why take a retreat?

Let's back up a bit and consider the question: Why take a personal retreat? There are countless reasons women are called or compelled to nurture them-selves in this way.

- During times of passage or celebration, stepping away from your routine can allow you to deeply experience and embrace a pivotal moment in your life.

- When profound change thrusts you into transition, a retreat can provide an opportunity to create a true compass for navigating that change.

- When you find yourself longing for a break, a timeout, or a few minutes by yourself, a retreat is just the thing to foster rest and renewal.

- When you find yourself asking "Who am I?", a retreat is the opportunity to allow your authentic self to be revealed.

- When you find yourself muttering the words "I am stuck," a retreat is a fabulous way to grease the wheels for forward motion, allowing the clarity that comes with moving off dead-center and leaving the familiar behind.

- Perhaps you are longing for a delicious window for creativity, for quiet, or for inspiration.

All of these reasons and more have *bask in a personal retreat* written all over them.

Your intention

As you plan your personal retreat, there is one critical ingredient to identify: what is your intention? A clear intention serves as an invitation to an extraordinary experience. Ask yourself: "What do I most long to experience while on retreat?" Create a simple statement that reflects that longing. As you make your plans, keep that intention close to your heart.

Where to retreat?

The next question is where to retreat? Choose the best ecosystem. Think about what your intention is for the retreat and choose a location that supports that intention. Be creative! Are you most longing for reflective time? What about a picnic by a lake or stream? Is getting clear about something at the heart of your desire to retreat? Why not find a location with a vista, a view? Most importantly, choose a place that feels nurturing and safe, a place in which you can breathe deeply and relax into your most comfortable self.

If you want to create mini-retreats throughout your week, think about crafting a special space within your home that is just for you. It could be a corner with a comfy chair and some personal treasures sprinkled about or a room dedicated just to nurturing you. The key is bringing your heart into designing this sacred space and clearly communicating its purpose to family members.

What will you do on retreat?

Mix a bit of creativity with your intention and see what unfolds. Perhaps you will find yourself sitting in a rocking chair being still; filling a journal-and-a-half or finding that no words make it on to the page; walking along a trail; lying in the grass watching clouds; howling at the moon; watching an ant hill; playing a new game; stretching your body or digging a hole into which you can lay issues to rest. Perhaps what occurs will be a surprise.

What to take on retreat?

This brings up the all important Retreat Kit. Craft yours to suit. Perhaps . . .

- A beautiful journal that inspires you to fill its pages.

- A stack of blank paper and some stationery (it can be a great time to write notes of gratitude).

- A few pencils and pens.

- A book of poetry and/or of inspiring words.

- Comfy clothes to accommodate the location and your mood – for sitting, hiking a trail, making sand castles, or venturing out in a rain shower.

- Healthy and simple munchies and food.

Don't be surprised if . . .

So you've heard the call, have your intention clear, your location set, and your Retreat Kit packed. Some stage-setting may be in order regarding the interesting and surprising voices that, at times, may whisper in your ear once you have begun. Your inner voice may come disguised in many shapes and sizes:

It may sing in one instance – *I am in heaven.*

In the next . . .

It may appear like the fog bank, obscuring what lies just to the other side.

It may declare: *I never want to go back . . .*

Only to coax you in the next moment to call it quits and go home early.

The voice of fear may say you are not worthy of this act of self-love and of letting your light shine, only to have the voice of love curl around you like a warm, fuzzy blanket reminding you how glorious you are.

You may delight in the words: *I am alone.*

Or you may murmur in this solitude: *I am lonely.*

Invite it all!

Be curious, be open, and be willing to be surprised. Sometimes you simply need to allow your inner voice to chatter a bit before it settles down. By allowing the observations to come up and flow by, you flush out the insecurities and soothe the nervousness that can come when you first give this unfamiliar gift to yourself. By saying and expressing a resounding YES to taking time on retreat, you are taking steps to reveal the path to your authentic self.

The ripple effect of incorporating retreat time into your life is far-reaching. It enhances the quality of your relationships, infuses your life with renewed energy and enthusiasm, and brings greater focus and clarity to each moment. With a creative spirit always invited into the mix, look for simple ways to bring retreating into your daily life.

Field Notes

What might get in the way of me taking
my very own personal retreat?

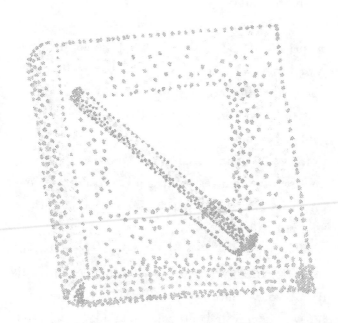

Field Notes

Brainstorm your ideal one-day retreat.
Paint the details in full color, then mark the date
on your calendar and make it happen.

Come to Your Senses

*"The voyage of discovery is not in seeking new
landscapes but in having new eyes."*
— Marcel Proust

Is your life flat or full? Is your life one-dimensional or multi-faceted? Do you see life in black and white or in technicolor? We often race so quickly through our lives that we forget to stop and smell the roses. A wise and inspired man by the name of Leonardo da Vinci once said, "The five senses are the ministers of the soul." One way to enrich our experience of each moment is to expand our ability to live through our senses. Once inspired as Leonardo was, we can literally come to our senses and marvel at the textures, tastes, and sounds that reveal themselves each and every day.

Think back for a moment and remember a time when you felt truly alive. What comes to mind when you recall that experience? Perhaps the tingling of

your skin, brilliant colors or the way light spar-
kled, a pulsing heart, a smell that curled into your
nostrils and transformed into deep satisfaction, or
a flavor that made your mouth pop! Your senses:
sight, sound, touch, taste, and smell are portals to
rich experiences. Spend time playing and rediscov-
ering the power of your senses and it will transform
the ordinary into the extraordinary in your life.

Get out of your head and into your body

Although you can read about the power of your
senses, your own experience will teach you the
benefits of living a more sensory life. Step One is
to literally get out of your head and into your body.
The following prompts and invitations may whet
your appetite, open new vistas, herald a call to dive
deep, tickle your soul to explore further, or invite
a delicious breath of new learning into your lungs
and heart.

Clear vision

Experience with clear vision what you see, instead
of interpreting. Once the colors, shapes, and images
become good or bad, pretty or ugly, familiar or

unfamiliar, you have stepped away from a clear view. Journal a sunset, an oak tree, or the moment at dusk when all is in shadow. You can take a glance and think, *nice*. Let your gaze linger and think, *Ahhh*. Describe it with your sense of sight in vivid detail. Do not stop until you have captured it all. Once you have set your pen down, read through your description. Notice how many details you would normally miss with a casual glance. What surprises can you find in your observation?

Another way to truly understand and gain clear vision is to practice seeing with eyes of love and wonder. Look into the face of someone you cherish. Invite them to share this experience. Spend several minutes in quiet observation and reverence. What can you learn about this beloved? What do you see that you have never seen before? How does your heart feel in response to such an intimate viewing?

Capture the music of your life

Look back on your life and discover what sounds still ripple in your memory. A puppy's excited bark, the sound of the 10 PM train, the melody of instruments from the kitchen as your mother prepared

Sunday breakfast, a cat's quiet purr, thunder rolling down off the ridge as a storm was approaching, a baby's giggle, or the sound of a deep breath. We don't always notice the nuances of sounds, but when we do, the moment is far richer. As you think back, feel the thrill of those sounds from days past coming full circle back around to you.

A great communication skill to master is to listen with your whole body to what someone is sharing: what resonates, what is compelling? That kind of intentional listening is a real gift to give and to receive.

Touch Awareness Day

You might think of the obvious: a warm hug, a firm handshake, a gentle massage; but how many things do you touch each day that you do not even notice? What if you simply went through one day paying attention to everything you touched, just noticing how everything felt? Create your very own Touch Awareness Day and expand your touch and watch for surprises. Expand your touch capacity even further by going through one day consciously touching everything with loving hands.

What tickles your taste buds?

How many meals have you had in the past week? How many bites did you really notice? How was the food prepared? Where did the food come from? Is it all a blur? Conduct a taste-testing extravaganza. Choose one of your all time favorite foods. Is it chocolate, fresh baked bread hot out of the oven, or a ripe and juicy pear? Make a meal of your favorite food and invite some friends over to join in this playful and one-of-a-kind picnic. Savor each bite, describe it and distinguish how one morsel differs from another.

The scent of inspiration

You breathe in and out all day and all night. Why not leverage each precious breath by noticing the scents they carry? Your sense of smell can inform, inspire, coax, and even caution you. A playful way to charge up your sense of scent is to make a savory meal and focus on how each portion smells *before* you taste.

Sight, sound, touch, taste, and smell are at the core of our physical and emotional experience.

With just a few exercises, you can dramatically enhance the depth, texture, and experience of your life. Wake up your senses, come to your senses and, in turn, you may fire up your passion in all areas of your life!

A recipe for a feast
(you create yours to suit)

Ingredients:

A few close friends

A table set with craft and care – fancy or simple

Candles – ah, yes, candles

Flowers, and beautifully scented – of course

First Course – Cream of Zucchini Soup – delicate and delicious, one spoonful at a time

And next – Rosemary Grilled Rainbow Trout, fresh salad, warm dill wheat rolls

And finally – one piece of exquisite dark chocolate

Oh and not to forget – a bottle of wine, clear sparking water

Each element carefully thought out

Each morsel mouth-watering

Each word spoken – spoken in the joy among friends

I have shared my feast with you . . . what will your feast include and when will your next feast be?

Field Notes

What kind of sensory picnic can you put together?

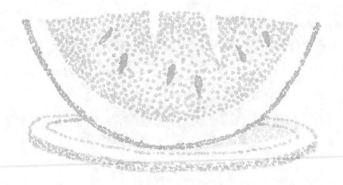

Field Notes

When I am in my head, I am missing out on the sensory experience of . . .

Beloved Treasure –
Your Body

"Living in our bodies means experiencing life through our feelings, sensations, and interaction and not simply from our projections and memories. When we begin to open and live in our body, whether through pain or joy, a whole new universe of alternatives becomes available to us."
— Richard Strozzi Heckler

Pretend for a moment you are a world-renowned photographer. You love your work and you are passionate about capturing each image you pull into focus in just the right way. At the end of each day you gently wipe off your camera and pack it away with the greatest of care. Periodically you give it a good cleaning and polish it up. It is through your camera that you express yourself, love each moment, and experience renewal each day in the surprises that show up in each frame. Because of this, you treat it as a beloved treasure.

Now shift your thinking. What if you were to treat your body with the same care and attention as the photographer treats that camera? Your capacity to live each moment to its fullest is ushered in through your body and how deeply you feel, see, sense; how your mind captures an idea and transforms it into action and how transforming your thoughts can transform your life.

What determines how resourceful you are? The greater your health, fitness, and mental dexterity, the greater your capacity to experience your life. Though some may be limited by physical restrictions, ailments, or emotional burdens, we each have the choice to make the body we have at this moment the best it can be.

There are countless books and resources for achieving optimal health because being a lifelong learner where your health is concerned is important. A potential pitfall is the complexity of much of the information.

Shave these written volumes down to their essence and you might just arrive at the "Simple is Do-able Model." In reality, the more complicated the information and model, the less likely you are to approach new behaviors. Play with this and see if it works for you.

The Simple is Do-able Model looks like this:

- Stretch when you wake up.

- Breathe deeply throughout the day.

- Eat simple and delicious foods and drink lots of pure, clean water.

- Exercise until you feel it deep within your body, a few times a week.

That isn't so radical, is it? If taking care of your body is a new idea, or you need occasional reminding just like me, start with one area and play there for a while.

Stretching is fun

Think about a cat first thing in the morning. It slowly gets up on all fours and then yawns and stretches out long. Cats feel delicious when they stretch. You can tell. Stretching first thing in the morning is a way to say, *Hello body*, and is a powerful way to build your body's resilience. The more flexible you are, the less likely you are to sustain injury and the more energy you feel. Take it further: a routine of stretching is a great reminder for you to practice openness and flexibility in your thinking. Getting stiff mentally and physically is painful and narrows your ability to experience the world.

You can stretch five or ten minutes a day or begin your day with a full routine of movement such as yoga. Whatever works is what you will actually take time to do.

Breath is life

When you are stressed-out or over-tired, how are you breathing? First of all, you probably are paying no attention, but if you were, it would likely be in short, shallow, tight breaths. Contrast that with a time you were completely relaxed. Your breath flows freely, deeply. Our bodies need oxygen and lots of it. Traditional and alternative medicines alike associate deep breath with reduced stress, greater energy, vitality, and health. Spending a few minutes each day in conscious, *through your nose and way down into your belly,* deep breathing is a great place to start.

Nourishment

Regarding food, there are so many theories and so many dietary plans that many people are overwhelmed. They therefore do nothing to improve their eating habits, or, in contrast, jump from one plan to the next. According to the *Simple is Do-able Model* here are the basic rules of thumb:

- Choose whole foods rather than highly processed foods.

- If you choose to eat meat, eat it in moderation.

- Consume organic whenever it is available. Toxic chemicals used to grow our foods end up in our foods and then end up in our bodies.

- Drink clean water. This rarely comes out of a tap unless you are blessed with wonderful spring water.

Oh, and I'll add, splurge occasionally, take time to enjoy each bite, give thanks for the availability of such wonderful food, and, in all things, practice moderation.

Get your heart going

Choose a form of exercise you enjoy. I repeat: choose a form of exercise you enjoy and move it onto your essential self-care priority list. Remember the photographer and his camera? If he left his camera in the case, several things might happen: he might lose his enthusiasm to pick it up, it might grow rusty, and it might become outdated.

Am I implying that might happen to your wondrous body if you do not use it? Absolutely! Walk, run, go to the gym, start a yoga practice, play tennis, ice skate, hike, join an aerobics class.

If you cannot answer the question: *What form of exercise do I enjoy doing,* then that is a great invitation to explore all kinds of options. Go with a friend to an exercise class; make one appointment with a personal trainer; ask a friend to become your walking buddy; strap on a set of cross-country skis. Keep exploring until you find one or more options that you will do at least two or three times a week. In every way – physically, mentally, energetically – you will feel better!

Taking great care of your body is an action, not a thought. One small action after another, throughout your day and throughout your life, adds up to what optimal health can be for you. With each action that supports vibrant health you are saying, *I am worth it!*

Field Notes

What things can I do right now
to take care of my body?

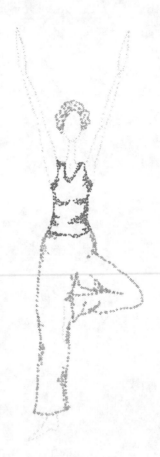

Field Notes

Pick one area: stretching, breathing, eating good food, or exercising and make one positive change for your health in that area today.

Making Mud Pies

"To be human is to be creative.
You don't have to go outside yourself to find
creativity — You already have it. It lives in your heart
and mind in every moment of every day."
— Sandra Magsamen

A downpour on a hot summer afternoon was always a call to action for my two children. As soon as the clouds parted and the sun came back out, they would spill out the door to do the inevitable — squishing bare toes in the ooze of soft dirt and making mud pies from a secret family recipe. A bit of this, some special gravel from the bank behind the house, a few leaves, an herbal powder of mashed greens plucked out of the garden with clenched hands and . . . Voila!

What made those times, and many times like them, so magical was the wild abandon with which my children created their masterpieces. No worries about doing it right or wrong, no concerns about messing up clothes, no hesitation to switch from one creation to the next when something cool caught their eye. The quality of curiosity, of wonder and of beauty in all their creative endeavors wafted in the air like an old time rose heavy with blooms.

It is interesting to note how easily creative freedom can slip past you as you grow older. You worry: *Gosh, how will I look? What will they think? What if I fail?* All these worries creep into your language and beliefs. The view of what is possible narrows, your resourcefulness to see past the obvious is dulled, and the creative spirit that pranced about unabashed gets tucked away in the shadows of a cobwebbed corner.

Rekindling that spark requires a call to action. In what ways can you entice your creativity, and with it greater joy, back out and into the light? How can you step past limiting beliefs and renew a childlike experience of creativity in your life? With intention – that's how!

Living an extraordinary life requires that you infuse it with a creative spark. The more intention you bring to nurturing creativity in your life, the more resourceful and playful you become. That's easy when you think of it this way: you are an original and you were from Day One. There is no one else like you on this entire planet. By showing up fully expressed, you are giving rise to a voice unlike any other. How, then, can we fan the flames of our uniqueness in a way that rekindles our spark and fuels a creative bonfire?

One approach would be to dig deep to reveal the baggage and beliefs that may be stifling your self-expression and to send them packing. Without jumping too quickly to a solution, how might you approach this differently – dare I say, with more creativity and more flair? An outside-the-box approach might be to forget about analyzing what gets in your way on this one and to simply step past it. With this shift you expand your resourcefulness and capacity to create new solutions.

Next, try having a conversation with yourself. Ask yourself:

- What activities make me feel joyful?

- What are great creative outlets for me?

- How might I feel if I were living a more creative life?

Then open the flood gates. As for me, I would play more music, dance more freely, learn to splash brilliant colors on a canvas, live and read and write more poetry, stitch a colorful line across colorful fabric, see more possibilities in every direction, inspire innovations, transform the ordinary in my life into the extraordinary, celebrate the artist in me, celebrate the artist in others, create amazing things, and live amazing experiences. What would you do?

Ingenuity, imagination, and creativity allow a glob of sticky mud to become a delicious and juicy pie and allow new insights and revelations to pop into the light. Coax your creativity out of the corner and celebrate its return home! At every turn think: *What would creativity have to say about this?* Sometimes the old approach is the best. Sometimes by simply asking a new question, you can blow the lid off what's possible. It can give you a charge, a thrill, a fresh perspective, a dose of fun.

A little secret from me: my kids weren't the only ones who loved making mud pies!

You choose . . .

A handful of words can make a poem

*A doodle on the edge of a scrap of paper
can make a drawing*

A twirl in the sunlight can make a dance

A hum while you fold clothes can be music

. . . You choose

Field Notes

Creativity in my life looks like . . .

Field Notes

One thing I will do today
to live a more creative life is . . .

Invite Others Over to Play

> *"Each friend represents a world in us,*
> *a world of possibility not born until they arrive,*
> *and it is only by this meeting that a new world is born."*
> *— Anans Nm*

Remember when . . . hop, skip, jump. "Ya wanna come over to play? We could climb the magnolia tree, ride our bikes, or go get an ice cream." Remember as a child, when playing with friends was like breathing air. You needed a good dose of playing with friends to feel connected, joyful, and adventuresome. As an adult you need a reminder to call up a friend to come over to play. Life gets busy, priorities get skewed and before you know it, you are thinking: it has been forever since I spent time with this person or that. Further, you need reminding to create fun opportunities to gather with friends. A conversation over a cup of coffee can be rich, and it doesn't have to stop there. What about a hike, a potluck, an invitation to go exploring for the day down country lanes or through an urban shopping jungle?

Here is a playful story . . .

Claire got a call from a girlfriend. She was invited to a get-together on Saturday night and was told to dress warmly in layers. Arriving at her friend's home she was asked, "So, do you want to know what we are going to do?" In true Claire spirit she said, "Oh no, surprise me." They hopped in the car and arrived shortly at the stables where her friend's horses were boarded. From the barn curled the scent of fresh, sweet-smelling straw and over the stalls peeked inquisitive horses. With a twinkle in her eyes, her friend spread a picnic blanket on the grass and cranked up her favorite music. She knew Claire loved to dance, and that night those two playful, wild women danced to their hearts content, barefoot, with horses smiling all around and with a canopy of stars above them. Now that was a creative invitation to come over to play!

We all want to connect with others, to feel truly seen and heard and honored for who we are, to belong to a community, a family. We want to give and receive love. This begins with how we show up, how we choose to nurture connections in our lives, and what our intention is. There may be times when we find ourselves feeling isolated and alone and wondering when our friends or family will come to call. There may be times when we look around and see only naysayers in our midst. As with all things in life, if our commitment is to live an exceptional life and we feel a lack of connection with others, then we have an opportunity to create new friendships and/or to revitalize old ones.

A powerful way to enhance the quality of your life is to enhance the quality of your relationships and to surround yourself with empowered, joyful folks. You know the ones: they exude vitality and warmth along the path they walk. They are like magnets and attract all kinds of magical people into their lives. If you were to capture the essence of them in a few words, they might be: positive attitude, no excuses, ability to listen well and express appreciation, lots of energy, vibrant, a can-do attitude, a deep sense of gratitude, and a willingness to extend a helping hand to others. Seek these people out and become one of them yourself. You will transform your life!

Seven simple ways to step up your life by stepping up relationships

1) Feeling a lack of appreciation from others? Express greater appreciation to others and do so in creative ways. Place a loving note under their pillow, wash and wax their car, or take them out for dessert.

2) Do you find yourself wishing you had more friends? Step out into the world in a way that provides new opportunities to connect with people who share your interests or hobbies. Join a book club, sign up for an exercise class, or ask someone you've just met out for lunch.

3) Get complete with all the people in your life. Is there something left unsaid, some conversation way overdue? If so, show up as your very best self and honor your relationship with honesty and care by getting complete on all fronts.

4) Seek out guides, mentors, and angels. Look for people who project sincerity and happiness and whose lives serve as beacons for inspired living. Ask them to be your mentor. It may seem a

stretch and yet the best way to learn something is often through inspired teaching and mentoring from others. Perhaps there are ways you can help them as they help you.

5) Exercise your smile muscle. A warm smile serves as an invitation to others and is a gift you can give freely throughout the day. One way to practice this is to play the following game: make a point of smiling every time you are talking on the phone. It is fun and really shifts your energy and the energy of the person on the other end of the line.

6) Take time out of your day to read about people living exceptional lives. What can you learn through their stories?

7) Create a massively supportive network of awesome people in your life. Who is on your team? A fabulous woman who always inspires your creative spirit; a gentle massage therapist whose touch is healing and nurturing; an expert in your field who welcomes your calls and inquiries? Identify your ideal support team and seek out folks who are honored to be a part of it and to have you as a part of theirs.

How does life feel when you are surrounded with people you cherish, who cherish you, and who inspire you to be the best you can be? Interact, engage, live the benefits that come when you are in nurturing and playful relationships. Choose your community wisely, show up, and delight in the revelation that having fabulous people in your life supports a fabulous you!

Sitting in a circle, women beside me; women across from me; women around me; women embracing me; women supporting me; women listening to me; women understanding me; women appreciating me; women admiring me; women comforting me; women laughing with me; women keening with me; women celebrating with me; women outraged with me; women creating with me; women allowing me to create my own way

Excerpt from
I Am a Woman Finding My Voice
By Janet Quinn, Ph.D., R.N.

Field Notes

In what ways can you be a better friend?
The rewards of being an incredible friend
are immeasurable.

Field Notes

Start a *Grateful-For-You* Campaign.
Reach out to your friends and family and
come up with creative ways to let them know how
grateful you are that they are in your life!

Navigational Tools for the Journey

A Change-Savvy Woman

"It is when we are in transition
that we are most fully alive."
— William Bridges

Change happens in our lives: dramatic, life-altering or subtle and small – it's inevitable. Sometimes it comes as an unexpected blow. Sometimes we invite change into our lives. There are the obvious events we associate with change: loss of a job, stepping into a new job, the beginning of a marriage, the ending of a marriage, a death, a birth, a move to a new home. Digging deeper, how about: a child leaving home, a change in health, a natural disaster, a new relationship, the transformation from one phase of life into another? Let's face it, living life means living through change. The fact is, the more dynamic our lives, the more we are growing and evolving and blossoming, and the more we are experiencing change. Learning how to success-fully navigate change and grow through the transi-tions in our life is a powerful life skill to master.

Feelings that accompany periods of transition in life can cover the spectrum from excitement and thrills to feeling overwhelmed and disoriented. While the earth beneath your feet may feel like it is constantly shifting, you may lose sight of what is up or down. You may feel an urgent need to grab control of the reins when you have no control.

Consider this: What might it feel like if you could more often flow with and through the chang-ing landscape of your life? What if you could develop the skill and finesse to masterfully navi-gate change, to become a Change-Savvy woman? How might that affect the quality of your life? Effective navigation requires a map of some kind and a starting point from which to get your bear-ings and set your course.

What follows is a seven-step process that you can apply again and again when you find change stirring things up. It can provide a clear path to walk and one that enhances your capacity to be in the moment and to find sure footing.

Step One: Observe what is

Slow down long enough to clearly observe what is happening. Honestly, realistically describe the situation.

Tip: This is often a great juncture at which to carve out some personal retreat time to reflect.

Step Two:
Create a climate for positive change

Take great care of yourself. Look for ways to rest and renew. Clearly communicate with those you love, what is happening and what support you may need.

Step Three: Visualize the ideal

Get clear about how you would like to emerge from this transition and how you want to feel. Capture it on paper. Extol the beauty of the place. Savor it.

Step Four:
Get comfortable being in the G.A.P.

A **G**lorious **A**dventure into **P**ossibilitites, that edgy place between where you were and where you are headed that is ripe with potential. So often we want to race through the GAP to get to what feels like the safety of the other side.

Notice that urgency when it arises and let it pass. The pause between here and there is a great time to allow the quiet whisper of your inner voice to be heard. You can then more effectively assess the strengths and resources at hand. Too, you can invite the shift from problem-solving to opportunity-harvesting.

Step Five:
Design a plan of innovative action

Clearly identify empowering steps to create movement forward and set up a system of accountability to sustain that forward momentum.

Step Six: Take action and lots of it

Shift out of your head and into motion, one step at a time.

Step Seven: Celebrate and evaluate!

Savor the causes for celebration, both the big ones and the little ones. Evaluate and readjust as your vision and action plan call for.

These seven simple steps provide a powerful navigational map. Contrast handling transitions with clarity and intention, lots of support, and, while taking great care of yourself, with reacting to whatever hits you next. The results are dramatically different. With a new tool, a new map in hand, your experience can become more grounded and rich with personal growth opportunities. You can let go of the need for certainty and relax into the unfolding process.

Change happens – it's inevitable! As a Change-Savvy woman, you have a greater capacity to step into the flow of your changing life and emerge more empowered by each new experience.

Field Notes

The biggest change
I am currently experiencing is . . .

Field Notes

The feelings I have about change are . . .

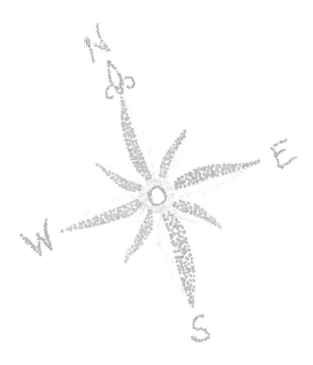

Become a Master Gardener

"The sculptor produces the beautiful statue by chipping away such parts of the marble blocks as are not needed – it is a process of elimination."
– Ebert Hubbard

Picture an overgrown field on an abandoned farm. Scattered about, you see rusty farm implements as well as bits and pieces of this and that. There is an old tractor that looks as if it dug its heels in one day right in the middle of furrowing a long row for corn and said: *That's it. I'm done.*

What once was a crisp patchwork of fields has become snarled with vines and thistles and little saplings boldly taking a stand.

Imagine it became your task, or even your passion, to tend this land, to reclaim this field, to grow a bountiful garden. How might you start?

One approach, and the quickest in response to your excitement, might be to push a few things aside, exposing enough dirt to drop in some seeds. *"I'll get to the other tasks later,"* you say. Give them a sprinkling of water and most likely you'd see a sprout before too long. Of course, there would be the weeds to contend with and the path you would have to maneuver around the old farm refuse to get to your plot. In your haste and excitement to get started, you might think past these potential obstacles in order to get your garden going. Over time, as tiny seedlings grow into garden goodies, the hours you spend keeping your path clear, keeping your plot free of invasive, curly, weedy things goes unnoticed. It becomes part of your routine.

Occasionally you look around you and think: *one day I'll haul that tractor off and one day I'll repair the fence and mow down the saplings that are taking over. For now, there just is not enough time. Funny how this little plot takes me all day to keep up with.*

Our lives often, before we notice, become like that overgrown parcel of land. We are working hard in one area to keep up, while the vines are covering up everything in other areas. We think: *if I could only get caught up.* The solution: become a master gardener.

How might a master gardener approach this scenario? First and foremost, she would create a master plan. Before picking the hoe up for the first time, she would step back and envision what she wants her garden to look and feel like. Based on that, she would identify the tasks at hand and create a strategy to bring life to her vision. It might look like this:

Clear the clutter — mow down the pastures, throw out the trash.

Delegate — any and all tasks that are appropriate.

Choose wisely. Say *No* often — which tasks support the vision, which are less pivotal? Say *No* often and clearly to keep the focus on track.

Though it may take a little longer to get seeds into the ground, when you have this kind of holistic approach, both your garden and your spirit will flourish.

Think about your life. Do you sometimes feel that if you could ever get caught up, it would be miraculous? Is there a sense that while you are working away on one front, things are getting out of hand on another?

If you take the time to step back and look at your life through the lens of a master gardener, what ways might you be able to tend to your life, to simplify and reap the bounty? Regardless of your current situation – just a few weeds popping up here and there or a tangled mess – the master gardener's tools can be sharpened up and brought out of the shed to do their work.

Stop! Long enough to take some deep breaths and to envision your ideal.

Clear the clutter: We can all use a big dose of simplification in our lives. A huge amount of time is spent stepping over and past and around all our "stuff." An easy way to begin this purge is to set aside the time and resources to do a thorough and literal cleaning in your life. From the filing cabinet to the kitchen cabinet to the closet shelves, go room to room, inside and out, clearing out that which does not support your ideal life. Hire a helper, enlist a friend. Work on this straight through or set aside fifteen minutes each day until it is done. To keep on top of this, create a *Clear the Clutter Day* each month or a few times a year. This is one of the most effective and powerful steps you can take in "lightening your load." It dramatically creates space, reduces distractions, and therefore allows you to focus in an empowered way.

Delegate: Ask for help. Tap into previously untapped resources. Invest in this process and you are investing in you!

Say No: An often overlooked and yet powerful way to prevent the invasion of clutter is to say *No*. Be clear on what you want and do not want, and say *No* more often. Clutter comes in many disguises. There is the kind that is spilling out of your basement door and there is the kind that shows up in a way-overbooked life.

Say *No* to friends who expect you to do things that are not on your list. Saying *Yes* to someone else means *No* to yourself.

We are all, no matter how deep and tangled the clutter feels, within reach of a lighter load and lighter life. A few decisions and a few actions can create miracles. How might it feel to have a life that is clear of clutter, well tended, and guided and guided by a master plan? It would feel lighter, more in the flow, as there would be fewer things blocking your path; and more exciting, as new windows of time and inspiration open up before you to do more of what you love.

Become the master gardener of your life. Clear your plot, look to friends and resources for help every step of the way, choose what you plant and what you pull out wisely, and reap the rewards of a bountiful harvest in all areas of your life.

We just moved into an amazing home. It was built over fifty years ago and about the time the walls went up a gardener, who must have had a twinkle in her eye, began tending the earth around her home. Laying little stone walls along the contour of the land, planting azaleas, rhododendron, camellias, gardenias, and countless shrubs and plants I have yet to identify.

Now, a half century later, the walls are ivy covered and appear the home of gnomes and fairies, the camillias are fifteen feet tall and bloom for months on end. Every day one plant loses its bloom something else pops open.

It likely did not happen all at once.
I imagine one seedling and one stone at a time.

Field Notes

Today I will begin to clear the clutter. I will . . .

Field Notes

The benefits to tending my life like a
master gardener would be . . .

Lessons from Your Past

"The past is a guidepost, not a hitching post."
— *L. Thomas Holdcroft*

As a woman with her eyes set on living a vibrant life, just what part does your past play? You often hear, *"Be in the present, define your vision, and look up and forward in the direction of your dreams."* There is no denying the value in that and yet there is no mention in those words of the power of cherishing your past. You hear, *"Let go of the past. That was then, this is now. Girl, get over it!"*

Two key facets of cherishing your past and therefore living fully in the moment are: having a sense of completion with the past and creating a spirit of gratitude that acknowledges that each step you have taken along your path has lead you to this moment. Without these, it's quite possible that you will find loose threads from your past tugging at your attention and distracting you from being fully here and now. In retracing your steps, perhaps it was a celebration that did not happen, words that were not spoken, or a loss that was not grieved. In what ways might you wrap up some unfinished business and more fully integrate all facets of your life experience?

A possibility to explore is that you can experience the lessons of your past in such a way that they inform, rather than dictate, how you show up in your world today. The past can be excavated with care, with gentle hands and heart, that tend like the soft tools of an archeologist brushing away the assumptions, the distorted memories, fears, and the moments of glorious celebrations. In that excavation, you can uncover a treasure trove of insights and revelations.

Integrate the elements and experiences that brought you to this day with who you are in this moment and who you are becoming. The closer your relationship is with your past, the greater your willingness to embrace, to grieve, to celebrate the trail of your life's passages; the greater will be your ability to live deeply, exceptionally in the here and now.

Your past is an inexact recipe, a bit of this, a bit of that, perhaps too little of this and way too much of that. Now that it is all in the mix, you cannot go back and correct or adjust your measurements. After all this time, the ingredients have mingled together and become something altogether different.

How then to explore and sort into neat piles your memories, your past? Therein lies the problem. You cannot. Those nice neat piles do not exist. If you can let go of that expectation and approach your past as an exciting new discovery into a vaguely familiar land, you can open up the possibility of insightful navigation, of blazing new trails, and of more empowered outcomes.

A question that may come up is: How to invite the past into your present life without allowing it to overstay its welcome? And, further, how to move through and release the sense of hold your past can claim? And, further still, how to celebrate your past in such a way that you reap the wisdom laced throughout its lessons?

Here are four guidelines:

- Be willing to try on a new line of inquiry.

- Be willing to invite new insights.

- Be open to unexpected answers.

- Be willing to reach out for support, as you may need it.

Keeping these touchstones in mind, how do you dive into the adventure of transforming your relationship with your past? Here is a powerful and effective process that calls for blank paper, some quiet time, and the courage to be radically honest. This can lead to a sense of completion, of richness and of freedom to move into the future of your life with a collection of treasures from your past. The premise: Transform your language to transform your experience.

Contrast a disempowering statement or question regarding your past with a possibility or *What if* question that instills a sense of growth and empowerment.

Here are some examples:

Disempowering statement:

I was too busy with life and I missed that very important moment.

Possibility question:

What if I slowed down long enough to celebrate that which I have yet to fully celebrate?

Disempowering question:

Why did that have to happen to me?

Possibility question:

What if I celebrated all the victories and hardships that have been and are my life and that make me who I am today?

Disempowering statement:

I know I can't change the past, but I can't seem to get over it.

Possibility question:

What if I step back into that place that feels incomplete and create a ritual to feel and experience it through to completion this time?

Disempowering statement:
If I look back, I'll have to feel that pain, and I do not want to.

Possibility question:
What if I allow myself to grieve that which I have not yet grieved?

Disempowering statement:
I used to dream about . . . and now the time for that has come and gone. It's too late now.

Possibility question:
What if I courageously uncover the dreams I buried in the compost along the way?

Take time to dive in. Notice your language, explore your language, and upgrade your language. Moving forward, each time you hear your inner voice murmur words of defeat, longing, or incompletion regarding your past, stop yourself and declare your *What if* . . . feel it, embrace it, notice it. It may call you to action or simply call your attention.

As you explore new language and a new relationship with your past, you may traverse some difficult trails. Be willing to honor yourself by reaching for support as you need it. It may be in the form of a friend, a therapist, or a warm and caring presence. Some journeys are yours to travel alone. Some call for a sacred circle of support. Let your heart lead you.

You cannot relive the past or change it, that's true. You can, however, transform how you are living your life today by excavating the treasures and the lessons from the path of your life up to this very moment. It all begins with awareness. Integrate the past. Invite it to come live in a nurtured place in your heart and feel a strengthened ability to be fully present and vibrant and fully expressed in the here and now.

Field Notes

I feel complete with my past
and here is how I will celebrate . . .
Or
I feel there is something tugging me from my past
and here is what comes to mind . . .

Field Notes

The most powerful Possibility Question I can craft regarding my past is . . .

Stepping Back
into the Flow

"You can't solve a problem with the same level of thinking that created the problem."
– Albert Einstein

Are you in motion with your life or do you find yourself stopped in your tracks, perhaps muttering the words *"I'm stuck"*? Stuck is a powerful word and evokes the feelings: *I can't move. My wheels are hung up in the sand. I've got a flat tire and there is no rescue in sight.* More importantly, stuck empowers the fear we may hold within us that says: "If I risk moving forward, through this, what will happen and can I handle it?" You might think, *I can handle stuck. It's familiar and there is very little risk, if any, involved in staying right here in this old familiar groove. Frankly, it is what is most convenient.*

Most everyone would have more fun being in the flow of their life, moving forward with clarity and excitement as each moment unfolds. That sticky Velcro feeling ends up being like a log jam in a river. To break up the log jam and step out of *stuck* and back into the current, it can be helpful to understand why you find yourself in a motionless state, unable to move forward, right or left, and unable to decide.

What are the benefits of being stuck? Here are just a few of the reasons that *stuck* takes a stand:

- You believe there are no good options, only limited options, or so many options you are overwhelmed.

- You simply cannot get clear enough to know what is best, so you are afraid to do anything at all.

- Old fears grab you by the throat and won't let you see your current life clearly.

- It may be your most familiar way of being in the world and resonates as home.

- The direction you may be heading is in conflict with your core values, and you pause with a sense that something doesn't feel right.

Any of these beliefs may contribute to a jammed-up, unable-to-budge kind of experience. The good news is that there are creative strategies to clear the way to get back into motion. If you have been standing in place long enough with *stuck* and are looking for a way to splash back into the flow, explore one or more of these exercises:

Free-flow the options

Gather some colored pencils and paper and doodle until you come up with every conceivable option and outcome. Usher your thoughts and ideas out of your head and onto paper. Let one idea lead to another: think radical and way outside-the-box, think practical and then allow yourself to think impractical until you have filled up a page. Do not edit and, once complete, walk away from your work. Let it percolate for a few hours, preferably a few days, and then come back. See what strikes you, what invites you, and be willing to be surprised by what happens next.

The power of a good question

Ask yourself the question, "What will it take to get clear about my next step?" Then make an action list. Talk to a neighbor; research a resource; build up a support network; practice a week of exceptional self-care; be willing to give up the need to be right and be willing to make a mistake.

A peek at the future

Contemplate the question: What will my life look like a year from now, five years from now, if I stay stuck? Paint that picture. Feel that edge.

Contrast the two

Take a piece of paper and divide it in two. At the top of one column right the words "My life as motion" and at the top of the other write: "My life as stuck." It is most likely that, while you may be stuck in one area of your life, there is movement and growth in other areas. List examples of areas in your life where you are growing and moving, as well as areas that feel *stuck*. Identifying that contrast can be eye-opening.

Get into motion in another area

Take radical self-affirming action in another area of your life to remind yourself that you can manifest movement and flow.

Stuck can be crafty. It can limit your movements and your view to such an extent that before you know it you have forgotten there is any other way of being in the world. Stagnation sets in, your senses dull, and your sense of life narrows down to just what is in view within the perimeter *stuck* has set, and thus you have excuses readily at hand. To get unstuck may take only the brush of a soft nudge, or it may take bold action, bold ownership, a willingness to invite play and, ultimately, courage to get back in motion again. You may need to dig deep, and in so doing, say hello to your fears. This threshold is often the precursor of growth and empowerment.

Play with this exploration and find yourself splashing back into the flow. You will be able to say thank you to *stuck* and wave goodbye as you welcome the revelation of new vistas coming into view just around the corner.

Field Notes

How does *Stuck* show up in your life?

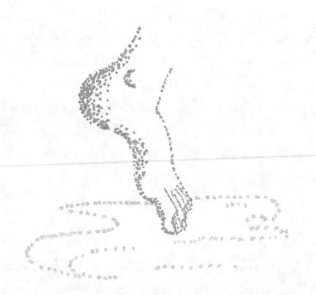

Field Notes

Pick one of the strategies to get Unstuck
and go for it . . .

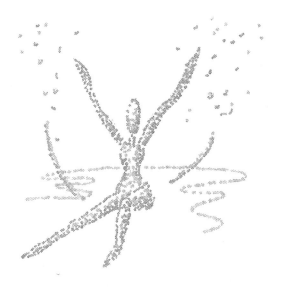

Touchstone Living

*"Your whole physical being knows that this
(following your passion) is the way to be alive in this
world and the way to give to the world the very best that
you have to offer. There is a track just waiting for each
of us, and once on it, doors open that were not open
before and would not open for anyone else."*
— Joseph Campbell

Touchstone living is about having clarity regarding who you want to be right now: what ways you want to shine and what you want to embody as you live this moment and move on to the next. What is a touchstone? It is a reference point and a quality or example that is used to test excellence or genuineness. Crafting your touchstone is the first step toward this type of living. In taking this step, you are heeding an adventurous call for self-exploration and discovery. Your touchstone is a statement of your vision for the future, crafted for the here and now. Why is this shift from *who do you want to be down the road in your ideal life* to *who do you want to be today* so very important? You clear a path for the life of your dreams by intentionally living your life as an expression of your dreams in each moment.

In the case of crafting your touchstone, Step One is to look forward to create a clear vision of what your most loved life would look like. Step Two then calls you back to the present to identify how you will show up, minute by minute, to embody your ideal life now. This clarity is informed by your vision, grounds you in who you choose to be in the here and now, and becomes your touchstone. With this in place, you have a point of reference to measure how you are actually living your life with your ideal way of being.

The shift is extraordinary

- Rather than "my life will be great when . . ." it becomes great now.

- Rather than being driven to create meaning in your life, you embrace living your life with meaning wholeheartedly.

- Rather than, "One day I'll manifest my ideal life," you understand that a perfect future unfolds from a perfect now.

Let's look to the process of defining a vision for your life. That centers around the question: "Who do you want to be?" In your inner dialogue, the natural pull is toward "What do I want to be, what do I want to do, and what do I want to have?" When you keep the focus on the *who,* you will be astounded at how the *what* unfolds in alignment with your desires.

A simple formula for embarking on this adventure is to ponder a few questions with your foot off the brake. Think expansive, think evocative, and think the sky's the limit. Give all limiting beliefs the day off and feel your way into your vision of a smile-filled, heart-full life.

Your ideal day

Take a deep breath . . . and one more . . . now . . . Imagine being in a place of deep satisfaction, your self-care cup is full, your life ripples with vibrancy and joy. With this in your heart and in your mind, describe what your ideal day would look and feel like. Imagine I have handed you a blank canvas and a box of paints in all the colors of the rainbow. Fill up the canvas and bring it to life in vivid detail. Who is in your life? Where are you? How do you spend each moment? How are you feeling? How are you showing up? Take all the time you need. Come back to this again and again to fill in things that pop into your mind, until the vision for your ideal day sparkles with clarity.

Living a life in alignment with your values

As the amazing Joseph Campbell so eloquently stated: "The privilege of a lifetime is being who you are." When you live a life aligned with your core values, you are connected, heart and soul, to living a meaningful life. It is that simple and true. The closer you are to living a life that expresses your values, the more satisfied you will find yourself. The farther away you are, the more you will experience the frustration of living an incongruent life.

How then to identify those values that resonate with the true you? Perhaps learning, creating, beauty, enthusiasm, inventing, compassion, nurturing, informing, excellence, discovering, contributing, honesty, integrity, comfort, connections, gratitude, sensitivity, humor, imagination, being fully expressed, and on and on. What pops up for you?

Brainstorm to come up with a handful of core qualities that resonate with you and fit like a glove.

A more adventuresome you

You've got your ideal day on your scope, have identified a few core values that speak to and of the authentic you, and now the most thought-provoking question: What would a life of no regrets look like?

When reflecting on all the discoveries to this point, both within this chapter and during your adventures throughout this book, think about this:

- Who do I want to be in this moment in order to be living an exceptional life?

- In what ways can I embody all the qualities I hold dear?

- How will I show up?

- How will I share the gifts of me with my world?

- And complete the following statement:
  I am a woman who . . .

Here are two examples crafted by empowered women. Use the framework or step way outside the box. Play with your language until it resonates deeply with you.

I am a woman whose passion is teaching people the skills needed for optimal health. I choose to show up with brilliance in each moment as the joy-filled teacher and healer that I am.

I am a woman whose passion is lifelong learning. I share the gift of me with the world by expressing my contagious enthusiasm for learning with each person that I touch.

Once complete, you have your touchstone. It becomes the invisible arms that hold you and nurture the best in you; an invisible hand that guides you effortlessly forward while living an authentic, open-hearted, exceptional life. It becomes one more navigational tool supporting you in living a life in alignment with your brilliance, a life that shines out as exceptional!

If I had my life to live over again, I wouldn't change a thing.

—Oliver Beirne Chisolm

Field Notes

My top ten ingredients for an ideal day are . . .

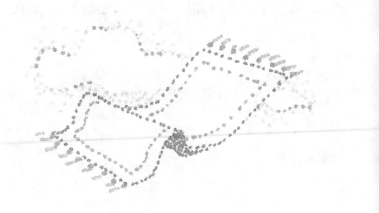

Field Notes

I am most deeply fulfilled when . . .

About the author

Corrie Woods is an author, Professional Life Coach, Speaker, and Women's Retreat Leader. As advocate, partner, collaborator, and "way-outside-the-box" thinker, Corrie challenges her clients to see the possibilities, to shift from negative to positive priority living, and to become vitally engaged in life. Working in collaboration with clients to dramatically expand the view of what's possible in living a fully expressed and fully loved life is Corrie's passion.

A bit of her collage ...

- Graduate, CoachU Coach Training Program

- Member, International Coach Federation

- Member of the *Retreat Coaches Network*

- Completion of Advanced Coach Trainings: The Art of Mindful Coaching with Doug Silsbee, PCC

- Certified *Seasons of Change* Facilitator

- MBTI, Myers-Briggs Personality Indicator administrator

- Participant, National Outdoor Leadership School

- Parent

- Poet

- Home Educator

About the illustrator

Caren Frost Olmsted has been drawing as long as she has been drawing breath. After graduating from college, she worked as a Theatre Designer and Art Teacher but having children rekindled her love of pictures and books. So in 2003 she swapped the chalkboard for the drawing board and has been a professional artist ever since. Caren's work has appeared on festival posters, commissioned paintings, the sides of buildings, and the interiors of books, as well as on The Learning Channel's hit show "Moving Up."

Caren lives in Basking Ridge, New Jersey with her husband and two sons (who are her most spectacular creations). Check out more of Caren's work at: www.cfodesign.com.

The aim of art is to represent not the outward appearance of things, but their inward significance.
—Aristotle

To Continue Your Journey Visit . . .
www.womansfieldguide.com

You will find tips, tools, and resources to support you in living an exceptional life.

At the website you can:
- Sign up for our free monthly e-newsletter: **Notes from the Field.**

- Explore the potential of a One-of-a-Kind Life Coaching Partnership crafted just for you.

- Browse free articles and resources.

- Learn about upcoming Retreats and Workshops.

- Contact Corrie.

An invitation: please share your stories. In what ways has this book enhanced your life? What one big *ah-ha* has happened for you? What discoveries have you found along the way? We love to hear back from readers and have our sights set on a collection of women's stories "from the field."

Tips for a
Woman's Field Guide™ Discovery Group

Magic happens when we come together as women in sacred space to grow, share, laugh, and explore our paths, our lives.

This book has been written from the perspective of the individual journey and yet can be expanded into a circle of women for even deeper inquiry.

Groups who may delight in experiencing the prompts together and and in sharing their insights and *ah-ha's:*

- Book Study groups

- Mom's night out groups

- Homeschool Moms groups

- Women on Retreat together

- Self-Care Support groups

. . . perhaps another group comes to mind for you.

Some suggestions

- For a change of pace from your group's routine, pick one chapter and have a lively discussion.

- Make a play day with your group around one theme

- Do Six Weeks Down the Trail – choose six topics and review one each week.

Key elements

- Safety: when we come together and share our stories with open hearts, it is vitally important that we feel safe. Ensure everyone agrees to confidentiality and everyone speaks from a place of support and caring.

- Keep the group small to ensure that everyone feels a part of the sacred circle.

- Be creative, have fun, celebrate your gathering!

BONUS

Ready for More?

To continue your adventure with The Woman's Field Guide™ and to receive your special bonus, go to:

http://www.womansfieldguide.com/bonus

You will receive The WFG Bonus Pack which includes:

- Crafting a Personal Retreat E-Booklet

- What if? Two Simple Words, Ten Powerful Questions, One Great Life – E-Booklet

- Become a ChangeSavvy Woman: Tip Sheet on the The ChangeSavvy Model for Inventive, Creative, and Empowered Change Along with Ten Tips to Become a ChangeSavvy Woman

- The Best of the Best WFG Newsletters – 12 issues of inspiration, resources and tips

All available to you in easy to view and download PDFs.

Printed in the United States
104288LV00001B/1-153/A